Easy
Science Experiments

by Diane Molleson and Sarah Savage
Illustrated by Heidi Petach

SCHOLASTIC INC.
New York   Toronto   London   Auckland   Sydney

For John, my favorite scientist
— D.M.

To Dad, for making this all possible
— S.S.

To my son Jeffrey, his friend Mike, and our dog Peaches,
who are all pictured on the sweet potato pages.
They are on one other page, too. See if you can find it!
— H.P.

ISBN 0-590-45304-1

Copyright © 1993 by Diane Molleson and Sarah Savage. Illustrations copyright © 1993 by Heidi Petach. All rights reserved. Published by Scholastic Inc.

12 11 10 9 8 7 6 5   3 4 5 6 7 8/9

Printed in the U.S.A.   24

First Scholastic printing, January 1993

Table of Contents

Experiments with

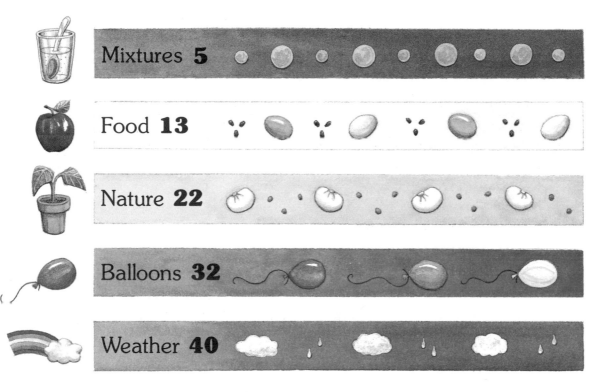

Scientists do experiments
to see how things work.
You can do experiments, too.

All you need are this book and materials
you can find around your house.
Have lots of fun!

*Try these experiments and see what
happens.*

MIXTURES

Make Salt Water

Add a spoonful of salt
to a glass of water.
Can you see the salt in the water?

Now stir the salt with a spoon.

Can you still see the salt?
What happened to it?

The salt is still there, but it is
in such tiny pieces you can't see it.
The salt dissolved in the water.

What else dissolves in water?

Make Lemonade

Try this same experiment with sugar.
Then add lemon juice to the water.
Stir this mixture with a spoon.
Does it dissolve in the water?

You have made a tasty mixture
you can drink.

Add Pepper to Water

Now take a spoonful of pepper
and add it to a glass of water.
Can you see the pepper?

Stir the pepper for about
thirty seconds.
Can you still see the pepper?

The pepper will not disappear
in the water. It will not dissolve.
The grains of pepper are lighter
than the water.
They float to the top.

Make a Fizzy Mixture

Try this experiment, too.
Pour some vinegar into an empty glass.

Now add a spoonful of baking soda
to the vinegar and stir it.
What happens?

You have made a mixture that bubbles.
Soon the baking soda will dissolve
in the vinegar.

When vinegar and baking soda mix,
they fizz and bubble because they are
changing to make something new.
They have combined to create a gas.

Find Out if Oil and Vinegar Mix

Mix some oil and vinegar in a glass.

Now stir and watch the oil break up into little drops.

When you stop stirring, the drops of oil rise.

Soon all the drops of oil
will rise and spread over the top
of the vinegar.
Can you guess why?

Oil and vinegar do not mix.
The oil is lighter than the vinegar
and floats on top.

FOOD

Make Vinegar Bread

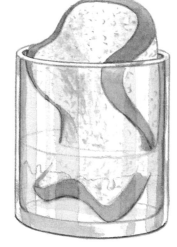

Stir the oil and vinegar again
with a spoon.

Dip a piece of white bread
in the mixture of oil and vinegar.
Leave the bread in the mixture
for a few seconds, then take it out.

Lick a little piece of the bread.
It will only taste of vinegar.
The white bread soaks
up the vinegar but not the oil.

Float an Egg

Gently drop an egg into a glass half full of water.
You can also use a hard-boiled egg
for this experiment.

The egg will fall to the bottom of the glass.

The egg is heavier than the water and
cannot float in it.
Now add two tablespoons of salt
to the water. Stir the water carefully
until *all* the salt dissolves.

What happens to the egg?

The egg will float in the water.

The salt water is heavier than
the egg, so the egg can float in it.

Soak Raisins in Water

Here's another experiment you can
try with salt water.
Fill two glasses with water.
Add two tablespoons of salt to one glass
and stir until the salt dissolves.

Now drop some raisins into both glasses.

Check the raisins after about an hour. What do you think will happen to the raisins?

The raisins in the plain water will swell. They will look puffier than the raisins in the salt water.

The raisins in the salt water will not change. They will stay small and wrinkled.

Make Raisins Dance

Fill a glass half-way with club soda or seltzer.
Quickly put five or six raisins in the glass,
one at a time.

Soon you will be able to see your raisins
move up and down, flip, and fall in the water.
Your raisins will be dancing.

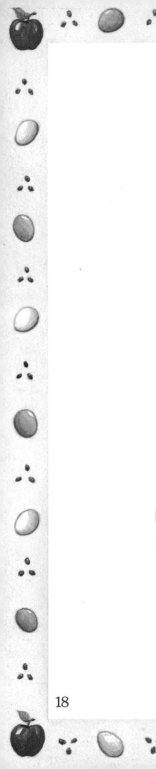

Soda bubbles are filled with gas.
When bubbles completely cover the raisins,
the raisins rise.
The bubbles make the raisins dance.

Put on some music and you can dance, too!

Taste Test

Hold a peeled onion up to your nose.
While you are smelling the onion,
bite into an apple.
How does the apple taste?

The apple tastes like an onion.
Your sense of smell is stronger than
your sense of taste.

Try tasting ice cream or biting into a
piece of chocolate while you smell
the onion.
What happens?

What Happens When You Put Salt on Apples?

Bite off two pieces of an apple
and put them on a plate.
Or have an adult cut them for you.
Sprinkle a little salt on one piece of apple.
Wait for a little while — about half an hour.

The salted piece will be covered with water.
The piece without salt will feel drier.

Try this experiment with pieces of
carrot, onion, or celery.
Does the same thing happen?

Fruit has water in it.
Water and salt like to mix.
The salt draws the water out of the fruit,
and dissolves in the water.

NATURE

Make Plants Grow

All you need are two large plastic cups
or clear glass jars, and seeds.

Lima beans, green beans, or radish seeds
are good for this experiment.
But you can use other kinds, too.

Line the glass jars or plastic cups
with a paper towel.
Now add about an inch of water
to the bottom of each jar.

Put the seeds between the jar and
the paper towel. Leave the seeds in
a warm place, like a sunny window ledge,
and keep about an inch of water at
the bottom of each jar.

In a few days, your seeds will sprout.
You will be able to see the roots
grow down in the jar, while the
stems grow upward.

When the roots get big, you can plant your
seeds in a pot with soil — or outside in dirt.
Remember to water your plant, and keep it
in a place where it can get sunlight.
A windowsill is a good choice.

23

Grow a Plant from a Sweet Potato

You can also grow a plant from a sweet potato.

Fill a tall clear glass with water.
Poke toothpicks on all sides of a sweet potato.
Place the sweet potato in the glass of water.
The toothpicks should rest on the rim of the glass.

They hold the sweet potato in the water,
but keep the top of the sweet potato dry.

In about a week, roots will begin to grow from the bottom of the sweet potato. Green leaves will start to grow from the top of the sweet potato.

Soon more and more leaves will grow from the top of the potato, and the roots will get bigger and bigger.

25

In a few weeks, you will have a
green leafy vine in your house.

When your vine gets big,
you can plant the potato in a pot with soil —
or you can leave the potato in the glass.

Make Celery Change Color

All plants need water to grow.
Water rises up the roots of a plant
to its leaves and petals.
It brings food from the soil to feed the plant.

Try this experiment to see how water
travels up the stalk of a vegetable.

Pour 6 ounces of water into a
tall glass or plastic cup.
Add fifteen drops of red or blue food
coloring to the water.
Stir the water with a spoon.

Now take a stalk of celery and snip off
the end with a pair of kitchen scissors.
Put the celery stalk in the colored water.

Leave the celery in the water for 48 hours.

The top of the celery will change color.
The celery stalk will be streaked with color.
Water rises from the roots of a plant to its leaves.
You can trace the colored water's path through
the celery's stalk.

Find Out How Plants Breathe

Plants also need air and light to grow.
Try this experiment to see how
plants get air and sunlight.
You need a green leafy
houseplant and some vaseline.

Put vaseline on the top sides of two leaves.
Now put vaseline under two other leaves.
Look at the leaves after one or two days.
What do you see?

The leaves with vaseline
under them will be dying.

Plants breathe through tiny holes
underneath their leaves.
The vaseline closes these holes
so no air can get through.

The plant needs sunlight, too.
Sunlight shines on the upper sides
of the leaves. The vaseline will not
block out the sunlight.

BALLOONS

Make a Balloon Boat

You should do this first balloon
experiment in your bathroom.
Fill the bathtub with water.
Blow up your balloon.
Hold the neck of the balloon
with your fingers.

Now, float the balloon in water.
Make sure to hold the neck
of the balloon out of the water.
Let go of the balloon.

Air shoots out of the balloon,
and the balloon boat goes forward.
When no more air comes out,
the balloon stops moving.

Make a Balloon Jet

You can also do this
experiment without water.
Blow up your balloon.
Hold it like this,
then let it go.

Your balloon goes up
into the air.
The air in the balloon
shoots down.

When no more air
comes out,
the balloon falls.

Pick Up Paper

For this experiment you will need your balloon, a woolen sweater, and small pieces of newspaper.

Blow up your balloon. Rub the balloon against the fuzzy sweater.

Now hold the balloon near the pieces of newspaper.

The newspaper will stick to your balloon.

When you rub a balloon with a woolen sweater, the balloon gets what we call an *electric charge*. The charge on the balloon attracts the pieces of paper. The balloon can pick up the paper because paper is so light.

What else can you pick up with your balloon?

A Magic Trick

Shake a pile of salt on a table.
Smooth it down with your fingers.
Shake pepper on top of the salt.

Now rub your balloon on
the fuzzy sweater.
Hold your balloon a little above
the salt and pepper mixture.
What happens?

The grains of pepper will jump
to the balloon.
Do you know why?

The grains of pepper are lighter than the grains of salt.

Freeze a Balloon

Blow up two balloons so they are about the same size. Tie the ends tightly with pieces of string so no air leaks out.

Put one balloon in the freezer. Keep the other balloon out.

After a whole day (24 hours), take the balloon out of the freezer. Hold it up next to the other balloon. What do you see?

The balloon in the freezer
got smaller.
The air inside the balloon
got colder.
Cold air takes up less space
than warm air.

Keep the cold balloon near the other balloon.
Soon it will be big again.
Soon it will be as big as the other balloon.

WEATHER

Freeze Water

In the last experiment,
you found out air takes up less space when it gets cold.
What do you think happens to water when it freezes?
You can see by doing this new experiment.

Pour some water into a plastic cup.
Put a piece of masking tape on the cup, and
mark the level of the water with a crayon.
(Make sure the cup is on a flat surface when
you mark it.)

Now freeze the water until it turns to ice.
Then look at the cup.
What do you see?

The ice takes up more room than the water.
Water takes up more space when it freezes.

Lift an Ice Cube

Here is an experiment you can do with
frozen water — ice cubes!

Put an ice cube in a glass filled with water.
Lay a piece of string across the ice cube,
as shown.
Sprinkle salt on top of the ice cube.

The salt will make the ice around the string melt a little.
After two minutes, lift the string.
What happens?

The ice cube will stick to the string.
When the ice around the string melted, it lost heat.
The ice cube was so cold, it made the water freeze again.

When it is icy outside, people sprinkle salt on the ice
to make it melt.

Make Water Disappear

Here is another experiment to try with water.
Pour water into a plastic cup until it is half full.
Put a piece of masking tape on the cup
and mark the level of the water.
Set the cup in a warm place and
leave it there overnight.

What happens to the water?

The level of the water is lower
because some of the water
disappeared into the air.

What do you think happens
to puddles of rain when it is
warm and sunny outside?

Look at Clouds

Clouds are tiny drops of water, or ice,
floating in the air.
Clouds help you guess what the weather will be.

Stratus clouds float low in the sky.
They bring rain or drizzle.

Cumulus clouds are big and puffy.
You can see them on clear sunny days.

Cirrus clouds float highest of all.
They are white and curly and look like scarves.
They bring a change of weather.

Go outside and look up at the sky.
What kinds of clouds do you see?

Make a Rainbow

Sometimes after it rains,
you can see a rainbow in the sky.
It may be hard to find a rainbow outside, but you
can make your own rainbow in this experiment.

Put some water in a baking pan.
Set the pan in sunlight coming through a window.
Now lean a small hand mirror against the inside of the pan.

You will see a rainbow on the wall or ceiling.

47

Look at all the colors in your rainbow — red, orange, yellow, green, blue, and violet. All these colors are in sunlight.

In sunlight these colors are mixed together. They look white. But when sunlight shines through water, the colors are separated. They come out one at a time. That is why you can see them.